Precision Financial Management

Comprehensive Techniques for Accurate Accounting
and Strategic Decision-Making

Eleanor J. Mitchell

Precision Financial Management

clarifying purposes only and are owned by the owners themselves, not affiliated with this document.

TABLE OF CONTENTS

Chapter 1: Introduction to Precision Financial Management

1.1. Understanding Financial Management

Financial management is the cornerstone of any successful business. It encompasses the planning, organizing, directing, and controlling of financial activities such as procurement and utilization of funds. Understanding financial management is imperative for anyone aiming to steer their business towards growth and sustainability. It involves a meticulous approach to managing the financial resources of an enterprise, ensuring that every dollar is used efficiently and effectively.

At its core, financial management is about making informed decisions that maximize the value of the business. This involves a delicate balance between risk and return, where the goal is to achieve the highest possible return with the least amount of risk. Financial managers must continuously assess the economic environment, market conditions, and the company's financial health to make strategic decisions.

One of the primary responsibilities in financial management is financial planning. This involves forecasting future financial needs and determining how best to meet those needs. Financial planning is not just about predicting expenses and revenues; it's about creating a roadmap for the company's financial future. This roadmap helps in setting realistic goals, allocating resources effectively, and preparing for potential financial challenges.

Budgeting is an integral part of financial planning. It involves creating a detailed plan that outlines how the company will spend its money over a specific period. A well-constructed budget helps in controlling expenditures, ensuring that the company does not spend more than it earns. It also aids in identifying areas where cost-saving measures can be implemented. Effective budgeting requires a thorough understanding of the company's operations and the ability to anticipate changes in the economic environment.

Another critical aspect of financial management is managing cash flows. Cash flow management ensures that the company has enough liquidity to meet its short-term obligations while also investing in long-term opportunities. This involves monitoring the inflow and outflow of cash, predicting future cash needs, and ensuring that there is always enough cash on hand to cover expenses. Effective cash flow management can prevent financial crises and enable the company to take advantage of investment opportunities.

Investment decision-making is another crucial component of financial management. It involves determining where to allocate the company's resources to achieve the best possible returns. This requires a thorough analysis of potential investments, considering factors such as risk, return, and the strategic fit with the company's overall goals. Investment decisions can range from purchasing new equipment to expanding into new markets or acquiring another company. Each decision must be carefully evaluated to ensure it aligns with the company's long-term objectives.

Financing decisions are equally important in financial management. These decisions involve determining the best mix of debt and equity to finance the company's operations and growth. The goal is to find the optimal capital structure that minimizes the cost of capital while maximizing shareholder value. This requires a thorough understanding of the different financing options available, such as issuing bonds, taking out loans, or selling equity. Each option has its own set of advantages and disadvantages, and the best choice depends on the company's financial situation and strategic goals.

Risk management is a critical part of financial management. It involves identifying, assessing, and mitigating financial risks that could impact the company's profitability and sustainability. This includes risks such as market fluctuations, credit risks, and operational risks. Effective risk management requires a proactive approach, where potential risks are identified early and strategies are put in place to mitigate them. This could involve diversifying investments, purchasing insurance, or implementing robust internal controls.

Financial reporting and analysis are essential for effective financial management. Accurate financial reports provide a clear picture of the company's financial health, enabling managers to make informed decisions. Financial analysis involves examining these reports to identify trends, assess performance, and make projections about future financial performance. Key financial statements such as the balance sheet, income statement, and cash flow statement are crucial tools in this process. They provide valuable insights into the company's financial position, profitability, and liquidity.

A deep understanding of financial management also involves staying abreast of changes in financial regulations and standards. Compliance with accounting standards such as

Generally Accepted Accounting Principles (GAAP) or International Financial Reporting Standards (IFRS) is essential for ensuring the accuracy and reliability of financial reports. Regulatory compliance also involves adhering to laws and regulations that govern financial activities, such as tax laws and securities regulations. Non-compliance can result in severe penalties and damage to the company's reputation.

Technology plays a significant role in modern financial management. Financial management software and tools can streamline processes, improve accuracy, and provide real-time insights into the company's financial status. These tools can automate tasks such as budgeting, forecasting, and financial reporting, freeing up time for managers to focus on strategic decision-making. Technology also enables better data analysis, allowing companies to make more informed decisions based on accurate and up-to-date information.

Effective financial management requires strong leadership and communication skills. Financial managers must be able to communicate complex financial information in a clear and understandable manner to stakeholders such as executives, employees, and investors. They must also be able to lead and motivate their team, ensuring that everyone is working towards the same financial goals. Strong leadership is essential for creating a culture of financial discipline and accountability within the organization.

In conclusion, understanding financial management is essential for the success of any business. It involves a comprehensive approach that includes financial planning, budgeting, cash flow management, investment decision-making, financing decisions, risk management, financial reporting, and compliance with regulations. Each of these components plays a critical role in ensuring that the company's financial resources are used efficiently and effectively, driving the business towards its strategic objectives.

Financial management is not just about managing numbers; it's about making strategic decisions that impact the overall health and growth of the business. It requires a deep understanding of both the internal dynamics of the company and the external economic environment. Financial managers must be adept at analyzing data, forecasting future trends, and making decisions that balance risk and return.

One of the key skills in financial management is the ability to interpret financial data. This involves not just looking at the numbers, but understanding what they mean in the context of the business. For example, a decline in revenue might indicate a problem with the company's sales strategy, or it might be due to external factors such as economic downturns. Financial managers must be able to analyze the data, identify the underlying causes, and develop strategies to address them.

Effective financial management also involves continuous learning and adaptation. The financial landscape is constantly changing, with new regulations, technologies, and market conditions emerging all the time. Financial managers must stay up-to-date with these changes and be willing to adapt their strategies accordingly. This requires a commitment to ongoing education and professional development, as well as a proactive approach to identifying and addressing potential challenges.

Ethical considerations are also a critical aspect of financial management. Financial managers have a responsibility to act in the best interests of the company and its stakeholders, which includes being honest and transparent in their financial reporting and decision-making. This involves adhering to ethical standards and practices, avoiding conflicts of interest, and ensuring that the company's financial activities are conducted in a fair and responsible manner.

In practice, financial management is a collaborative effort. It involves working closely with other departments within the company, such as operations, marketing, and human resources, to ensure that financial goals are aligned with the overall business strategy. This requires strong communication and teamwork skills, as well as the ability to build effective relationships with colleagues and stakeholders.

One of the challenges in financial management is dealing with uncertainty and risk. No matter how carefully a financial plan is crafted, there will always be unforeseen events and changes in the marketplace that can impact the company's financial performance. Financial managers must be prepared to navigate these uncertainties, using their skills and experience to make informed decisions and adjust their strategies as needed.

In summary, understanding financial management is a multifaceted endeavor that requires a combination of technical skills, strategic thinking, and ethical judgment. It involves managing the company's financial resources in a way that supports its long-term goals, while also ensuring compliance with regulations and maintaining the trust of stakeholders. Effective financial management can drive business success, enabling the company to achieve its objectives and create value for its shareholders. By mastering the principles and practices of financial management, individuals can play a pivotal role in guiding their organizations towards sustained growth and profitability.

1.2. Importance of Precision in Accounting

Precision in accounting is the bedrock upon which the reliability of financial information rests. Accurate accounting practices are essential for making informed business decisions, complying with regulatory requirements, and maintaining the trust of stakeholders. Inaccuracies in financial records can lead to misguided decisions, financial losses, and legal troubles, making precision an indispensable aspect of accounting.

Imagine a small business owner, Emma, who meticulously tracks every transaction in her bakery. She records each sale, every purchase of ingredients, and all operational costs. This diligent record-keeping allows Emma to understand her bakery's financial health at any given moment. She knows which products are most profitable, when to reorder supplies, and how to price her goods competitively while maintaining a healthy profit margin. Emma's success is a testament to the importance of precision in accounting.

Errors in accounting can have far-reaching consequences. For instance, overstating revenues or understating expenses can present an inflated view of financial performance, misleading investors and other stakeholders. This was notably illustrated in the early 2000s with major corporate scandals like Enron and WorldCom, where accounting inaccuracies and fraudulent reporting led to massive financial collapses and loss of investor confidence. These cases underscore the critical need for accuracy and transparency in financial reporting.

Precision in accounting also facilitates effective budgeting and forecasting. Accurate financial records provide a solid foundation for creating realistic budgets and reliable financial forecasts. When businesses have precise data on past performance, they can make better predictions about future revenues and expenses. This enables them to allocate resources efficiently, plan for growth, and anticipate potential financial challenges.

Consider a manufacturing company that relies on precise accounting to manage its inventory. By maintaining accurate records of raw materials, work-in-progress, and finished goods, the company can optimize its production processes and reduce waste. Precise inventory accounting helps the company avoid stockouts and overproduction, both of which can have significant financial implications. It also ensures that the company can meet customer demand without unnecessary delays.

Tax compliance is another area where precision in accounting is crucial. Accurate financial records are essential for calculating tax liabilities correctly and ensuring that businesses pay the right amount of taxes. Errors in tax reporting can lead to penalties, interest charges, and even audits by tax authorities. By maintaining precise accounting records, businesses can avoid these issues and ensure that they remain in good standing with tax authorities.

Moreover, precision in accounting is vital for securing financing. Lenders and investors rely on accurate financial statements to assess the financial health and creditworthiness of a business. Inaccurate or incomplete financial records can hinder a company's ability to obtain loans or attract investment.

Financial institutions require detailed and precise financial information to evaluate the risks associated with lending or investing in a business. Therefore, businesses that prioritize precision in their accounting practices are more likely to secure the funding they need for growth and expansion.

Internal controls play a significant role in achieving precision in accounting. These are processes and procedures implemented by a company to ensure the accuracy and reliability of its financial information. Internal controls include measures such as segregation of duties, regular reconciliations, and approval processes for financial transactions. By implementing robust internal controls, businesses can minimize the risk of errors and fraud, ensuring that their financial records are precise and trustworthy.

Technology has greatly enhanced the ability of businesses to achieve precision in accounting. Accounting software and systems automate many of the tasks that were once done manually, reducing the likelihood of human error. These tools can perform complex calculations, generate financial reports, and maintain accurate records with a high degree of precision. Additionally, cloud-based accounting systems provide real-time access to financial data, enabling businesses to make timely and informed decisions.

Training and education are also critical components of achieving precision in accounting. Accountants and financial professionals must stay updated with the latest accounting standards, regulations, and best practices. Continuous professional development ensures that they have the knowledge and skills necessary to maintain accuracy in their work. Businesses should invest in training programs for their accounting staff to ensure that they are proficient in using accounting software and understand the importance of precision in their roles.

Ethics in accounting cannot be overlooked when discussing precision. Ethical accounting practices ensure that financial information is reported honestly and accurately. Accountants must adhere to ethical principles such as integrity, objectivity, and professional competence. By maintaining high ethical standards, accountants can ensure that their financial records are precise and reliable, fostering trust and credibility with stakeholders.

The importance of precision in accounting extends beyond the individual business to the broader economy. Accurate financial reporting is essential for the efficient functioning of capital markets. Investors, regulators, and other stakeholders rely on precise financial information to make informed decisions. Inaccurate accounting can distort market perceptions, leading to misallocation of resources and potential financial instability. Therefore, precision in accounting contributes to the overall health and stability of the financial system.

In conclusion, precision in accounting is fundamental to the success and sustainability of businesses. It ensures that financial information is accurate, reliable, and useful for decision-making. Precise accounting practices enable businesses to manage their finances effectively, comply with regulatory requirements, and maintain the trust of stakeholders. By prioritizing accuracy in their accounting processes, businesses can achieve greater financial stability and make more informed strategic decisions. The ripple effects of precision in accounting are felt across all facets of a business, from daily operations to long-term planning, and ultimately, to its reputation and relationships with stakeholders.

1.3. Strategic Decision-Making in Financial Management

Strategic decision-making in financial management is a critical function that shapes the long-term success and sustainability of any business. It involves the careful analysis of financial data, market trends, and business objectives to make informed choices that drive growth and profitability. Effective strategic decision-making requires a blend of analytical skills, foresight, and a deep understanding of the financial landscape.

Consider the case of a mid-sized manufacturing company, Horizon Industries, which faced the challenge of declining sales and rising production costs. The company's leadership team, recognizing the need for strategic intervention, embarked on a comprehensive analysis of their financial data. They reviewed sales trends, cost structures, and market dynamics to identify the root causes of their financial woes. This analytical approach provided the insights needed to make strategic decisions that would reposition the company for growth.

One of the first steps in strategic decision-making is to establish a clear understanding of the company's financial health. This involves conducting a thorough financial analysis, including the examination of key financial statements such as the income statement, balance sheet, and cash flow statement. These documents provide a snapshot of the company's financial performance and position, highlighting areas of strength and weakness. For Horizon Industries, this analysis revealed that while their revenue streams were robust, their profit margins were being eroded by inefficient production processes and high operational costs.

Armed with this knowledge, the leadership team at Horizon Industries set out to develop a strategic plan. They identified cost reduction as a key objective and explored various options to achieve this goal. One of the options considered was the adoption of lean manufacturing principles to streamline production processes and eliminate waste. This decision required careful evaluation of the potential benefits and risks, as well as the investment needed to implement these changes.

Strategic decision-making also involves evaluating different scenarios and their potential impact on the business. This is where financial forecasting and modeling come into play. By creating financial models, businesses can simulate various scenarios and assess their potential outcomes. For Horizon Industries, modeling different cost reduction strategies helped them determine the most effective approach. They projected the impact of lean manufacturing on their production costs, profit margins, and overall financial performance. This analysis provided the confidence needed to proceed with the implementation of lean principles.

Another critical aspect of strategic decision-making is the consideration of external factors. Market conditions, competitive landscape, regulatory environment, and economic trends all play a significant role in shaping financial decisions. Horizon Industries, for instance, monitored market trends to identify opportunities for growth. They noticed a rising demand for eco-friendly products and decided to invest in sustainable manufacturing practices. This strategic decision not only aligned with market trends but also enhanced the company's reputation and competitive positioning.

Risk management is an integral part of strategic decision-making in financial management. Every strategic decision carries inherent risks, and it is crucial to identify, assess, and mitigate these risks. Horizon Industries conducted a comprehensive risk assessment to identify potential challenges associated with their strategic initiatives. They evaluated risks related to supply chain disruptions, implementation challenges, and financial uncertainties. By developing contingency plans and risk mitigation strategies, they were able to navigate these challenges effectively.

One of the most challenging aspects of strategic decision-making is balancing short-term needs with long-term goals. Businesses often face pressure to deliver immediate results, but it is essential to consider the long-term implications of strategic decisions. For Horizon Industries, the decision to invest in lean manufacturing and sustainable practices required significant upfront investment. However, the long-term benefits in terms of cost savings, improved efficiency, and enhanced market positioning justified the investment. Strategic decision-making involves a careful consideration of the trade-offs between short-term gains and long-term sustainability.

Communication and collaboration are also vital components of strategic decision-making. Effective decision-making requires input and alignment from various stakeholders within the organization. Horizon Industries established cross-functional teams to collaborate on their strategic initiatives. By involving representatives from finance, operations, marketing, and other departments, they ensured that diverse perspectives and expertise were considered. This collaborative approach facilitated buy-in and commitment from all stakeholders, enhancing the likelihood of successful implementation.

The role of technology in strategic decision-making cannot be overlooked. Financial management tools and software provide valuable insights and enable data-driven decision-making. Horizon Industries leveraged advanced analytics and business intelligence tools to analyze their financial data and gain deeper insights into their operations. These tools helped them identify trends, forecast future performance, and evaluate the impact of different strategic options. Technology-enabled decision-making provided a competitive edge by enhancing the accuracy and speed of their strategic analysis.

Continuous monitoring and evaluation are essential to ensure the success of strategic decisions. Once a strategic decision is implemented, it is crucial to track its progress and measure its impact. Horizon Industries established key performance indicators (KPIs) to monitor the effectiveness of their lean manufacturing and sustainability initiatives. Regular reviews and performance assessments allowed them to make necessary adjustments and ensure that their strategic objectives were being met.

In conclusion, strategic decision-making in financial management is a multifaceted process that requires a combination of analytical skills, foresight, and collaboration. It involves a thorough analysis of financial data, consideration of external factors, risk assessment, and a balance between short-term needs and long-term goals. Effective strategic decision-making also relies on the integration of technology and continuous monitoring to ensure the effectiveness and alignment of strategic initiatives with the overall business goals. The case of Horizon Industries illustrates the importance of a structured approach to strategic decision-making, where careful analysis, scenario planning, and stakeholder collaboration lead to informed and impactful financial decisions.

Understanding key concepts and techniques in financial management is crucial for anyone looking to navigate the complex world of business finance. These foundational elements provide the tools and frameworks necessary for effective decision-making and strategic planning. Imagine a small business owner, Emma, who runs a local bakery. She's passionate about her craft but struggles with the financial aspects of her business. By grasping essential financial concepts and techniques, Emma can transform her bakery into a thriving enterprise.

The first key concept in financial management is the time value of money (TVM). This principle states that a dollar today is worth more than a dollar in the future due to its potential earning capacity. For Emma, understanding TVM means she can make better decisions about investing her profits or taking loans. She learns that by investing her earnings in a high-interest savings account, she can grow her money over time, rather than letting it sit idle.

To complement TVM, discounted cash flow (DCF) analysis is a crucial technique. DCF helps in valuing an investment by estimating its future cash flows and discounting them to present value. Emma uses DCF to evaluate whether expanding her bakery to a new location would be a wise investment. By projecting future cash flows from the new location and discounting them back to present value, she can assess whether the expansion will provide a satisfactory return on investment.

Another fundamental concept is the distinction between profit and cash flow. Profit refers to the financial gain after all expenses are subtracted from revenue, while cash flow represents the actual inflows and outflows of cash. Emma realizes that even if her bakery shows a profit on paper, she might still face cash flow problems if her receivables are not collected promptly. Understanding this difference helps her manage her finances more effectively, ensuring she always has enough cash to cover her expenses.

Budgeting is an essential technique for financial management. A budget is a financial plan that estimates income and expenses over a specific period. For Emma, creating a budget allows her to plan for future expenses, such as purchasing new baking equipment or hiring additional staff. By comparing actual performance against her budget, she can identify areas where she is overspending and take corrective action.

One of the most critical concepts in financial management is risk management. Every business decision carries some level of risk, and managing that risk is vital for long-term success. Emma learns to identify potential risks, such as fluctuations in ingredient prices or changes in consumer preferences. She then develops strategies to mitigate these risks, such as securing long-term contracts with suppliers to lock in prices or diversifying her product line to appeal to a broader customer base.

Leverage is another key concept that involves using borrowed funds to finance business operations. While leverage can amplify returns, it also increases risk. Emma considers taking out a loan to renovate her bakery, weighing the potential benefits against the increased financial burden. By understanding her debt-to-equity ratio, she ensures that she does not overextend herself financially.

To evaluate her bakery's financial health, Emma employs various financial ratios. Liquidity ratios, such as the current ratio and quick ratio, measure her ability to meet short-term obligations. Solvency ratios, like the debt-to-equity ratio, assess her long-term financial stability. Profitability ratios, including the net profit margin and return on assets, indicate how well her bakery is generating profit from its operations. These ratios provide a comprehensive view of her business's financial condition and help her make informed decisions.

Cost-volume-profit (CVP) analysis is another valuable technique. CVP helps businesses understand how changes in costs and sales volume affect profit. Emma uses CVP to determine the break-even point for her bakery, where total revenue equals total costs. This analysis helps her set sales targets and pricing strategies to ensure profitability.

Capital budgeting is a technique used to evaluate long-term investment decisions. Emma considers purchasing a new commercial oven to increase her bakery's production capacity. Using techniques like net present value (NPV) and internal rate of return (IRR), she assesses the potential returns from this investment. NPV calculates the difference between the present value of cash inflows and outflows, while IRR identifies the discount rate that makes the NPV of an investment zero. These techniques help Emma decide whether the investment is worthwhile.

Diversification is a risk management strategy that involves spreading investments across different assets to reduce risk. Emma diversifies her revenue streams by offering catering services and selling baked goods online. This strategy helps protect her business from market fluctuations and ensures a steady income.

Understanding financial statements is fundamental for financial management. The three primary financial statements are the income statement, balance sheet, and cash flow statement. The income statement shows the bakery's profitability over a specific period, detailing revenues, expenses, and net income. The balance sheet provides a snapshot of the bakery's financial position at a given point in time, listing assets, liabilities, and equity. The cash flow statement tracks the flow of cash in and out of the business, highlighting operating, investing, and financing activities. By regularly reviewing these statements, Emma gains insights into her bakery's financial health and performance.

Working capital management is another crucial concept in financial management, encompassing the management of a company's short-term assets and liabilities to ensure operational efficiency and financial stability. For Emma, managing working capital involves balancing her bakery's inventory levels, accounts receivable, and accounts payable. By optimizing inventory, she avoids tying up too much cash in stock while ensuring she has enough ingredients to meet customer demand. Efficient accounts receivable management ensures timely collection from customers, improving cash flow. Similarly, managing accounts payable allows her to take advantage of supplier terms without compromising cash flow.

2.1. The Accounting Cycle: From Transactions to Statements

Every business, regardless of size or industry, relies on accurate financial records to make informed decisions. The accounting cycle, a systematic process of identifying, recording, and processing financial transactions, ensures these records are accurate and comprehensive. To illustrate the importance of this cycle, let's follow Sarah, a small business owner, who runs a boutique clothing store. By understanding and implementing each step of the accounting cycle, Sarah can maintain her store's financial health and make strategic decisions for growth.

The accounting cycle begins with the identification of transactions. These transactions can be anything that affects the financial position of Sarah's boutique, such as sales, purchases, or expenses. Sarah diligently keeps track of every sale she makes, whether it's a cash transaction or a credit sale. She also records every purchase of inventory and any expenses incurred, such as rent and utilities. By thoroughly identifying these transactions, Sarah ensures that no financial event is overlooked.

Once transactions are identified, they must be recorded in a journal, a process known as journalizing. Sarah uses double-entry bookkeeping, where each transaction affects at least two accounts. For example, when she sells a dress for $100, she records a debit to the cash account and a credit to the sales revenue account. This method maintains the accounting equation: Assets = Liabilities + Equity. Sarah's diligence in recording every transaction ensures her financial statements will be accurate.

The next step in the accounting cycle is posting journal entries to the ledger. The ledger is a collection of accounts that shows the changes made by each transaction. Each journal entry is transferred to the relevant accounts in the ledger. Sarah posts her journal entries regularly, updating her cash account, sales revenue account, inventory account, and expense accounts. This step organizes her financial information, making it easier to summarize and analyze later.

After posting to the ledger, Sarah prepares an unadjusted trial balance. This is a list of all her accounts and their balances at a specific point in time. The purpose of the unadjusted trial balance is to ensure that total debits equal total credits, confirming the accuracy of the bookkeeping. Sarah carefully reviews her trial balance, checking for any discrepancies. If she finds that debits do not equal credits, she investigates and corrects any errors before moving on.

Adjusting entries are the next crucial step in the accounting cycle. These entries are made at the end of an accounting period to update account balances before preparing financial statements. Adjusting entries ensure that revenues and expenses are recognized in the period they occur, following the matching principle. For instance, Sarah adjusts for any prepaid expenses, such as insurance or rent, that have been used up during the period. She also records depreciation on her store's equipment and adjusts for any accrued expenses or revenues. These adjustments provide a more accurate picture of her boutique's financial position.

With the adjustments made, Sarah prepares an adjusted trial balance. This document reflects all account balances after the adjusting entries have been posted. Like the unadjusted trial balance, the adjusted trial balance ensures that total debits equal total credits. Sarah reviews this balance carefully, knowing it forms the basis for her financial statements.

The preparation of financial statements is the next step in the accounting cycle. Sarah prepares the income statement, which shows her boutique's revenues and expenses over a specific period, resulting in net income or loss. She then prepares the balance sheet, which provides a snapshot of her boutique's financial position at a specific point in time, detailing assets, liabilities, and equity. Finally, she prepares the statement of cash flows, which shows how cash has flowed in and out of her business, categorized into operating, investing, and financing activities. These financial statements provide valuable insights into her boutique's performance and financial health.

After preparing the financial statements, Sarah makes closing entries to reset the balances of temporary accounts, such as revenues and expenses, to zero. This process ensures that these accounts are ready to capture transactions for the next accounting period. Closing entries transfer the net income or loss to the owner's equity account. For Sarah, this means transferring her net income to the retained earnings account, reflecting the increase in her boutique's equity due to profitable operations.

Following the closing entries, Sarah prepares a post-closing trial balance. This document lists all permanent accounts and their balances after the closing entries have been made. The post-closing trial balance ensures that total debits still equal total credits and confirms that the temporary accounts have been properly closed. Sarah reviews this balance to ensure the accuracy of her books as she prepares for the next accounting period.

Throughout the accounting cycle, Sarah uses various tools and techniques to maintain accuracy and efficiency. She employs accounting software to automate many of the repetitive tasks, such as posting journal entries and preparing trial balances. This software reduces the risk of human error and saves time. Sarah also regularly reconciles her bank statements with her ledger to catch any discrepancies early. By comparing her bank statement with her cash account, she ensures all transactions have been recorded correctly and that her cash balance is accurate.

Internal controls are another critical aspect of the accounting cycle. These controls help prevent errors and fraud, ensuring the integrity of Sarah's financial information. She establishes segregation of duties, where different individuals handle different aspects of transactions. For example, one employee might handle cash receipts while another records these transactions in the accounting system. This separation reduces the risk of errors and fraud. Sarah also implements regular internal audits, where she or an external auditor reviews her financial records for accuracy and compliance with accounting standards.

2.2. Double-Entry Bookkeeping: Ensuring Balance

Double-entry bookkeeping, a cornerstone of modern accounting, offers a robust method for maintaining financial accuracy and transparency. This system, which dates back to the 15th century and was popularized by the Italian mathematician Luca Pacioli, ensures that every financial transaction affects at least two accounts, keeping the accounting equation—Assets = Liabilities + Equity—in balance. To illustrate the practical application and importance of double-entry bookkeeping, let's follow the journey of Carlos, an entrepreneur who owns a small tech startup.

Carlos's startup, Tech Innovations Inc., is growing rapidly, and as the complexity of the business increases, so does the need for a reliable accounting system. Double-entry bookkeeping becomes a vital tool for Carlos to track his company's financial health accurately. At the heart of this system is the concept of debits and credits. Every transaction is recorded in two parts: a debit in one account and a credit in another, ensuring the total debits always equal the total credits.

For example, when Tech Innovations Inc. makes its first sale of $10,000, Carlos needs to record this transaction. The sale increases the company's revenue and its cash on hand. Therefore, he debits the Cash account for $10,000 and credits the Sales Revenue account for the same amount. This transaction shows that the company has more cash due to increased sales revenue, maintaining the balance in the accounting equation.

Carlos also needs to purchase equipment for his startup. He buys computers worth $3,000 on credit. This transaction affects both the Equipment account and the Accounts Payable account. Carlos debits the Equipment account, increasing it by $3,000, and credits the Accounts Payable account by the same amount, reflecting the liability. This entry ensures that the total assets and total liabilities remain balanced.

A crucial aspect of double-entry bookkeeping is understanding the nature of debits and credits. Debits increase asset or expense accounts and decrease liability, equity, or revenue accounts. Conversely, credits increase liability, equity, or revenue accounts and decrease asset or expense accounts. Carlos initially finds this concept confusing, but with practice, he becomes proficient in applying it correctly to various transactions.

Each transaction in double-entry bookkeeping is recorded in a journal, also known as the book of original entry. Carlos maintains a general journal where he records all transactions in chronological order. Each journal entry includes the date, accounts affected, amounts debited and credited, and a brief description of the transaction. This detailed record-keeping helps Carlos trace each transaction back to its source, providing a clear audit trail.

After recording transactions in the journal, Carlos posts them to the ledger, a collection of accounts that show changes to each account's balance. The ledger is organized into different accounts, such as Cash, Accounts Receivable, Equipment, Sales Revenue, and Accounts Payable. By posting journal entries to the ledger, Carlos can see the cumulative effect of all transactions on each account. For instance, after several sales and purchases, the Cash account in the ledger will reflect the net increase or decrease in cash.

To ensure the accuracy of his records, Carlos prepares a trial balance periodically. The trial balance is a list of all ledger accounts and their balances at a specific point in time. It serves as a checkpoint to verify that total debits equal total credits. If they do not, Carlos knows there's an error that needs to be investigated and corrected. This step is crucial for maintaining the integrity of the financial statements.

Double-entry bookkeeping also plays a significant role in preparing financial statements. The income statement, which shows the company's revenues and expenses over a period, is derived from the revenue and expense accounts in the ledger. The balance sheet, which provides a snapshot of the company's financial position, is based on the asset, liability, and equity accounts. By ensuring that every transaction is recorded in two places, double-entry bookkeeping provides the foundation for these critical financial reports.

As Carlos's startup grows, he hires an accountant, Maria, to manage the increasing volume of transactions. Maria appreciates the double-entry system because it provides internal controls that reduce errors and prevent fraud. For example, if someone tries to manipulate the books by altering one side of a transaction, the imbalance in debits and credits will reveal the discrepancy. This built-in check makes double-entry bookkeeping a reliable method for ensuring financial integrity.

Maria also uses accounting software to streamline the bookkeeping process. The software automates many tasks, such as posting journal entries to the ledger and preparing trial balances. It also generates financial statements with a few clicks, saving time and reducing the likelihood of errors. However, Maria knows that understanding the principles of double-entry bookkeeping is essential, even with software, as it helps her interpret and verify the automated entries.

The versatility of double-entry bookkeeping extends beyond just recording transactions. It also aids in financial analysis and decision-making. For instance, by analyzing the ledger, Maria can identify trends in Tech Innovations Inc.'s expenses, such as increasing costs for research and development. This insight allows Carlos to make informed decisions about budgeting and resource allocation. Similarly, tracking accounts receivable and accounts payable helps Carlos manage cash flow more effectively, ensuring the company has sufficient liquidity to meet its obligations while maximizing opportunities for investment and growth.

2.3. Key Financial Statements: Balance Sheet, Income Statement, and Cash Flow Statement

Understanding key financial statements is pivotal for anyone venturing into the world of accounting or managing a business. These statements provide a comprehensive view of a company's financial health, performance, and cash flows, enabling informed decision-making. To illustrate their significance, let's follow the experiences of Sarah, a small business owner managing a bakery called "Sweet Delights."

Sarah has always been passionate about baking, and her dream of owning a bakery came true two years ago. However, as her business grows, she realizes that understanding and managing her finances is as crucial as creating delicious pastries. Sarah's accountant, John, introduces her to the three primary financial statements: the balance sheet, the income statement, and the cash flow statement. Each statement offers unique insights into different aspects of her business's financial status.

The balance sheet, also known as the statement of financial position, provides a snapshot of Sweet Delights' financial standing at a specific point in time. It is divided into three main sections: assets, liabilities, and equity. John explains that assets are what the bakery owns, including cash, inventory, equipment, and receivables. Liabilities represent what the bakery owes, such as loans, accounts payable, and other debts. Equity reflects the owner's interest in the business, calculated as the difference between assets and liabilities.

For instance, at the end of the year, Sarah's balance sheet shows total assets of $150,000, including $20,000 in cash, $50,000 in inventory, and $80,000 in equipment. On the liabilities side, she has a $40,000 loan and $10,000 in accounts payable, totaling $50,000. The equity section shows that Sarah's equity is $100,000 ($150,000 in assets minus $50,000 in liabilities). This balance sheet gives Sarah a clear picture of her bakery's financial resources and obligations, helping her assess its net worth.

Next, John introduces Sarah to the income statement, also known as the profit and loss statement. This statement summarizes the bakery's revenues, expenses, and profits over a specific period, typically a month, quarter, or year. It starts with total revenues, then subtracts the cost of goods sold (COGS) to find the gross profit. Operating expenses like rent, utilities, salaries, and marketing are then deducted from the gross profit to calculate the operating income. Finally, interest, taxes, and other non-operating items are considered to determine the net income.

Sarah's income statement for the past year shows total revenues of $300,000 from sales of pastries and cakes. The COGS, which includes the cost of ingredients and direct labor, amounts to $120,000, leaving a gross profit of $180,000. Her operating expenses, including rent, utilities, and wages, total $100,000. After subtracting these expenses, the operating income is $80,000. Finally, after accounting for taxes and interest, the net income stands at $60,000. This income statement helps Sarah understand how profitable her bakery is and where she might need to control costs or increase revenues.

The third key financial statement John explains is the cash flow statement. Unlike the income statement, which focuses on profitability, the cash flow statement tracks the actual inflows and outflows of cash within the bakery. It is divided into three main sections: operating activities, investing activities, and financing activities. Operating activities include cash transactions related to the bakery's core business operations, such as receipts from sales and payments to suppliers and employees. Investing activities cover cash flows from buying or selling assets like equipment. Financing activities involve cash received from or paid to investors and creditors, such as loan proceeds and repayments.

For Sweet Delights, the cash flow statement reveals that the bakery generated $70,000 in positive cash flow from operating activities, reflecting strong sales and efficient expense management. However, Sarah invested $30,000 in new baking equipment, which appears in the investing activities section. Additionally, she repaid $10,000 of her loan, shown under financing activities. Despite these outflows, the net cash flow for the year is positive at $30,000, indicating that the bakery has sufficient cash to support its operations and future growth.

Sarah quickly realizes that each financial statement provides valuable insights, but their true power lies in how they complement each other. The balance sheet shows the bakery's financial position at a specific moment, while the income statement reveals its profitability over time. The cash flow statement bridges the gap between these two by showing how cash moves in and out of the business, highlighting the liquidity and solvency of Sweet Delights.

By regularly reviewing these financial statements, Sarah can make more informed decisions about her bakery. For example, when considering whether to expand her product line, she can use the income statement to evaluate potential profitability, the balance sheet to assess whether she has sufficient assets to support the expansion, and the cash flow statement to ensure she has the necessary liquidity to fund the project.

Understanding these statements also helps Sarah communicate effectively with stakeholders such as investors, lenders, and suppliers. For instance, when Sarah approaches a bank for a loan to expand her bakery, she can present her financial statements to demonstrate the bakery's stability and growth potential. The balance sheet will show the bank her current assets and liabilities, the income statement will highlight her profitability, and the cash flow statement will provide evidence of her ability to manage cash effectively.

2.4. Maintaining Accuracy: Common Pitfalls and How to Avoid Them

Accuracy is the bedrock of effective accounting. For beginners, maintaining accuracy in financial records can be challenging due to the complexities of accounting processes and the potential for human error. To illustrate, let's delve into the journey of Mark, a novice accountant at a mid-sized manufacturing firm. Mark's experiences highlight common pitfalls in accounting and provide practical strategies for avoiding them.

Mark's first major task is to prepare the monthly financial statements for his company. Eager to impress, he dives into the pile of invoices, receipts, and bank statements. However, he quickly realizes that ensuring every transaction is recorded accurately is more challenging than he anticipated. One common pitfall he encounters is data entry errors. These errors, whether due to typographical mistakes or misinterpretation of data, can significantly skew the financial statements.

For example, Mark mistakenly records a $5,000 payment as $500. This seemingly small error results in a substantial discrepancy in the company's cash balance, which could lead to misguided financial decisions. To mitigate data entry errors, Mark adopts a double-entry system, where every transaction is recorded in at least two accounts. This method not only ensures balance but also provides a built-in error-checking mechanism. Additionally, Mark uses accounting software with validation checks that prompt him to review entries that appear unusual or inconsistent.

Another common pitfall Mark encounters is the improper categorization of expenses. Accurate financial reporting relies on correctly classifying expenses into appropriate accounts. Initially, Mark struggles with differentiating between operating expenses and capital expenditures. For instance, he incorrectly classifies the purchase of new machinery as an operating expense rather than a capital expenditure. This misclassification affects the company's profit and loss statement and its balance sheet, leading to inaccurate financial analysis.

To avoid such pitfalls, Mark creates a detailed chart of accounts that clearly defines each category and provides examples of typical transactions. He also consults with senior accountants and refers to accounting standards to ensure he understands the correct classifications. Over time, this practice not only improves the accuracy of his financial reporting but also enhances his understanding of the company's financial structure.

Timing is another critical aspect where inaccuracies can arise. Mark learns that recording transactions in the wrong accounting period can distort financial results. For instance, if he records a revenue transaction in December that actually pertains to January, it inflates the year-end figures and misrepresents the company's performance. To prevent such issues, Mark implements a strict cut-off policy, ensuring that all transactions are recorded in the correct period. He also reconciles accounts at the end of each month to catch any timing discrepancies early.

Reconciliation itself is an essential practice that helps maintain accuracy. Mark discovers that regularly reconciling bank statements, accounts receivable, and accounts payable with the general ledger is crucial. During one reconciliation, he notices a discrepancy between the bank statement and the company's cash account. Upon investigation, he finds that a customer's payment was recorded but not deposited in the bank. This early detection allows him to correct the error before it escalates.

Mark also learns the importance of maintaining proper documentation. In his early days, he occasionally misplaces receipts or fails to attach supporting documents to transactions. This oversight creates challenges during audits and makes it difficult to verify the accuracy of financial records. To address this, Mark implements a systematic filing system, both digitally and physically, ensuring that every transaction is supported by appropriate documentation. He scans and uploads receipts, invoices, and contracts, linking them to corresponding entries in the accounting software. This practice not only enhances accuracy but also streamlines the audit process. error is an inevitable part of accounting, but Mark realizes that regular reviews and audits can mitigate its impact. He sets up periodic internal audits where he and his colleagues review each other's work. These peer reviews help catch errors that may have gone unnoticed and provide an opportunity for collaborative learning. Mark also seeks feedback from external auditors, who offer an unbiased perspective on the accuracy and completeness of the financial records.

Another pitfall Mark encounters is the complexity of tax regulations. Initially, he struggles to apply the correct tax codes and rates to different transactions. Misapplication of tax rules can lead to underpayment or overpayment of taxes, resulting in penalties or lost funds. To avoid this, Mark attends tax training sessions and keeps updated with changes in tax laws. He also uses tax software that integrates with the accounting system, ensuring that the correct tax treatments are applied automatically.

Maintaining consistency in accounting methods is also crucial for accuracy. Mark realizes that changing accounting methods or estimates arbitrarily can create confusion and inaccuracies. For example, switching depreciation methods mid-year without proper documentation and rationale can lead to inconsistent financial reporting. To maintain consistency, Mark adheres to the company's accounting policies and procedures, documenting any changes and ensuring they are justified and approved by senior management.

Communication plays a vital role in maintaining accuracy. Mark often collaborates with other departments to gather financial data. He finds that miscommunication or lack of information can lead to errors. For instance, if the sales department fails to inform him about a large order that was canceled, it can result in overstating revenue or inventory levels. To mitigate this risk, Mark establishes regular communication channels with other departments. He sets up monthly meetings with department heads to discuss any significant transactions or changes that could impact financial reporting. By fostering a culture of open communication, Mark ensures that he receives timely and accurate information, reducing the chances of errors due to miscommunication.

2.5. Case Study: Small Business Accounting Best Practices

Sarah had always dreamed of opening her own bakery. With a passion for creating delectable pastries and a small loan from her family, she launched "Sweet Delights" in the heart of her hometown. However, like many small business owners, Sarah quickly realized that managing her bakery's finances was just as critical as perfecting her recipes. Through trial and error, she learned several best practices for small business accounting that ensured her bakery's financial health.

One of Sarah's first challenges was setting up an efficient bookkeeping system. Initially, she used a simple spreadsheet to track her expenses and income. While this worked for a few months, as her business grew, the spreadsheet became cumbersome and error-prone. She decided to invest in small business accounting software, which automated many of the processes and provided real-time financial insights. This transition not only saved her time but also reduced the likelihood of manual errors.

To keep her financial records organized, Sarah established a habit of daily bookkeeping. Every evening after closing the bakery, she would spend half an hour entering the day's sales, expenses, and any other financial transactions into the accounting software. This routine ensured that her records were always up-to-date and accurate, making it easier to monitor her cash flow and identify any discrepancies early.

Cash flow management was another crucial aspect Sarah had to master. In the initial months, she often found herself scrambling to cover expenses because she underestimated the importance of maintaining a steady cash flow. She started creating weekly cash flow forecasts, which helped her anticipate periods when cash might be tight and plan accordingly. For example, she noticed a pattern where ingredient costs spiked every few weeks due to bulk purchases. By planning for these expenses and setting aside funds in advance, she avoided cash shortages and ensured she could always meet her obligations.

One of the best practices Sarah adopted was separating her personal and business finances. At first, she used her personal bank account for business transactions, which made it difficult to track her bakery's financial performance accurately. She opened a dedicated business bank account and obtained a business credit card. This separation not only simplified her accounting but also provided a clearer picture of her bakery's profitability and financial status.

Sarah also learned the importance of maintaining detailed records of all her financial transactions. She kept copies of receipts, invoices, and bank statements, both in digital and physical formats. This thorough documentation was invaluable during tax season and when preparing financial reports. It also provided a safety net in case of audits or disputes with suppliers or customers.

Tax compliance was another area where Sarah had to educate herself. As a small business owner, she was responsible for understanding and fulfilling various tax obligations, including sales tax, payroll tax, and income tax. She decided to consult with a professional accountant who specialized in small businesses. The accountant helped her navigate the complexities of tax regulations and ensured she took advantage of all available deductions and credits. This professional advice not only saved her money but also gave her peace of mind knowing that her taxes were handled correctly.

Inventory management was a critical component of Sarah's accounting practices. She needed to know exactly how much inventory she had on hand to avoid overstocking or running out of essential ingredients. She implemented an inventory tracking system that integrated with her accounting software. This system allowed her to monitor inventory levels in real-time and automatically update her financial records as inventory was purchased or used. By keeping accurate inventory records, Sarah was able to reduce waste, manage costs more effectively, and ensure she always had the necessary ingredients to meet customer demand.

Pricing her products correctly was another challenge Sarah faced. She needed to ensure her prices covered all her costs while remaining competitive. She calculated her pricing by considering the cost of ingredients, labor, overhead, and desired profit margin. She also analyzed her competitors' pricing to ensure her products were priced appropriately within the market. Periodically, she reviewed her pricing strategy to account for changes in costs or market conditions, ensuring her bakery remained profitable.

Payroll management was essential as Sarah hired additional staff to support her growing business. She needed to ensure her employees were paid accurately and on time while complying with payroll regulations. She utilized payroll software that integrated with her accounting system, automating the calculation of wages, taxes, and deductions. This automation reduced the likelihood of errors and saved her significant time.

Additionally, she set up a process for regularly reviewing payroll reports to ensure accuracy and compliance.

As her bakery expanded, Sarah recognized the importance of financial reporting. Regularly generating and reviewing financial reports, such as profit and loss statements, balance sheets, and cash flow statements, provided her with a clear understanding of her bakery's financial health. These reports helped her make informed decisions about budgeting, investing in new equipment, and identifying areas for cost savings. She scheduled monthly meetings with her accountant to review these reports and discuss any financial concerns or opportunities.

Sarah also understood the value of budgeting and financial planning. She created an annual budget that outlined her expected revenues, expenses, and profits. This budget served as a financial roadmap, guiding her business decisions and helping her stay on track to meet her financial goals. She regularly compared her actual financial performance to her budget , adjusting her plans as needed to address any deviations. This proactive approach allowed her to manage her resources effectively and ensure that her bakery remained financially stable.

Chapter 3: Advanced Financial Techniques

3.1. Revenue Recognition: Principles and Practices

Revenue recognition is a cornerstone of financial reporting, ensuring that a business accurately reflects its financial performance. Understanding when and how to recognize revenue can be challenging, especially for beginners. To illustrate the principles and practices of revenue recognition, consider the journey of a fictional company, GreenTech Innovations, a startup focused on eco-friendly home appliances.

GreenTech Innovations, founded by Elena, was gaining traction rapidly. The company's flagship product, a solar-powered water heater, was in high demand. However, as sales increased, so did the complexity of their financial reporting. Elena soon realized the importance of understanding revenue recognition principles to ensure her financial statements were accurate and compliant with accounting standards.

The core principle of revenue recognition is that revenue should be recognized when it is earned and realizable. This means that revenue is recorded when goods or services are delivered to the customer, and there is reasonable assurance that payment will be received. For GreenTech Innovations, this meant recognizing revenue at the point when their water heaters were delivered and installed in customers' homes, not when the order was placed or the payment was received.

To delve deeper into this principle, it's essential to understand the five-step model introduced by the Financial Accounting

Standards Board (FASB) and the International Accounting Standards Board (IASB) under the Accounting Standards Codification (ASC) 606 and International Financial Reporting Standard (IFRS) 15. This model provides a comprehensive framework for revenue recognition across various industries.

The first step is to identify the contract with a customer. For GreenTech Innovations, a contract could be a written agreement, a purchase order, or even an implied arrangement based on customary business practices. The key is that the contract establishes the rights and obligations of both parties. Elena ensured that all customer agreements were documented clearly, specifying the terms and conditions of the sale.

The second step is to identify the performance obligations in the contract. A performance obligation is a promise to transfer a distinct good or service to the customer. In GreenTech's case, the primary performance obligation was the delivery and installation of the solar-powered water heater. However, if the contract included additional services, such as maintenance or extended warranties, these would also be considered performance obligations.

The third step involves determining the transaction price, which is the amount of consideration the company expects to receive in exchange for fulfilling its performance obligations. This step can be straightforward when the price is fixed, but it becomes more complex with variable considerations, such as discounts, rebates, or performance bonuses. Elena had to carefully evaluate any potential variable considerations to ensure an accurate transaction price.

The fourth step is to allocate the transaction price to the performance obligations. If the contract includes multiple performance obligations, the total transaction price must be allocated based on the standalone selling prices of each obligation. For GreenTech, this meant separately valuing the water heater, installation services, and any additional maintenance agreements. Allocating the transaction price accurately ensures that revenue is recognized proportionately as each performance obligation is satisfied.

The fifth and final step is recognizing revenue when the performance obligation is satisfied. Revenue is recognized either over time or at a point in time, depending on the nature of the obligation. For GreenTech Innovations, revenue from the sale and installation of water heaters was recognized at a point in time—specifically, upon completion of installation. However, revenue from maintenance services would be recognized over time, as the services are provided.

One practical challenge Elena faced was dealing with advance payments. Customers often paid a deposit when placing an order, with the balance due upon installation. According to revenue recognition principles, advance payments should not be recognized as revenue until the related performance obligation is satisfied. Instead, these payments are recorded as deferred revenue, a liability on the balance sheet, until the installation is complete.

Another complexity arose with sales returns and allowances. Occasionally, customers returned products or requested partial refunds for various reasons. To handle these situations, GreenTech Innovations estimated the expected returns and created a provision for sales returns. This provision reduced the amount of revenue recognized and ensured the financial statements accurately reflected potential future liabilities.

Elena also had to consider the impact of warranties. GreenTech offered a standard one-year warranty on its products, included in the sales price. Since the warranty was an assurance-type warranty, it did not represent a separate performance obligation. However, any extended warranties sold separately were treated as distinct performance obligations, with revenue recognized over the warranty period.

To ensure compliance with revenue recognition standards, Elena implemented robust internal controls and accounting policies. She established procedures for reviewing contracts, identifying performance obligations, and allocating transaction prices. Regular training sessions and updates kept her accounting team informed about the latest standards and best practices.

Additionally, Elena leveraged accounting software that supported the five-step model of revenue recognition. This software automated many aspects of the process, from tracking contracts and performance obligations to calculating transaction prices and recognizing revenue. The automation reduced the risk of errors and streamlined the financial reporting process.

As GreenTech Innovations expanded its product line and entered new markets, Elena encountered more complex revenue recognition scenarios. For instance, the company started offering subscription-based services for remote monitoring and maintenance of their solar-powered appliances. This introduced a new layer of complexity in revenue recognition.

3.2. Expense Management: Controlling Costs Effectively

Expense management is a fundamental aspect of maintaining financial health and ensuring the sustainability of any business. For small businesses, in particular, controlling costs can mean the difference between thriving and merely surviving. Let's dive into the principles and practical strategies of effective expense management through the lens of a fictional small business, Artisan Coffee Roasters, founded by Michael and Clara.

Artisan Coffee Roasters began as a passion project for Michael and Clara, who shared a love for high-quality, ethically sourced coffee. As their business grew, they quickly realized the importance of managing expenses to maintain profitability and support their mission. Their journey provides valuable insights into the practices of controlling costs effectively.

One of the first steps Michael and Clara took was to conduct a thorough review of their expenses. They categorized their costs into fixed and variable expenses. Fixed expenses, such as rent and salaries, were relatively stable and predictable. Variable expenses, such as raw materials and utilities, fluctuated with the level of production and sales. Understanding this distinction helped them identify areas where cost-saving measures could be implemented.

A detailed budget became their primary tool for expense management. They created a budget that projected their monthly income and expenses, allowing them to set financial targets and monitor their performance. This budget was not static; they reviewed and adjusted it regularly based on actual performance and changing business conditions. By comparing their budgeted expenses to actual expenses, they could quickly identify variances and take corrective actions.

One effective strategy for managing variable expenses was negotiating with suppliers. Michael and Clara built strong relationships with their coffee bean suppliers, which allowed them to negotiate better prices and payment terms. They also explored bulk purchasing options and long-term contracts, which provided cost savings and price stability. Additionally, they regularly reviewed their supplier agreements to ensure they were getting the best possible deals.

Another area of focus was inventory management. Overstocking inventory tied up valuable capital and increased storage costs, while understocking could lead to stockouts and lost sales. Michael and Clara implemented an inventory management system that tracked stock levels in real time. This system allowed them to optimize their inventory levels, reduce carrying costs, and improve cash flow. They also adopted a just-in-time inventory approach for some items, minimizing excess stock and reducing waste.

Michael and Clara recognized the importance of efficient operations in controlling costs. They analyzed their production processes to identify any inefficiencies or waste. By streamlining workflows and implementing best practices, they were able to reduce labor costs and improve productivity. For example, they invested in training their staff to operate more efficiently and adopted lean manufacturing principles to minimize waste and maximize resources.

Energy consumption was another significant expense for Artisan Coffee Roasters. Michael and Clara conducted an energy audit to identify areas where they could reduce energy usage and lower utility bills. They invested in energy-efficient equipment, optimized their roasting schedules to off-peak hours, and implemented simple measures like turning off lights and machines when not in use. These efforts not only reduced costs but also aligned with their commitment to sustainability.

Controlling marketing and advertising expenses was also crucial. Michael and Clara leveraged low-cost digital marketing strategies, such as social media, email marketing, and content marketing, to reach their target audience. They tracked the performance of their marketing campaigns to ensure they were getting a good return on investment. By focusing on cost-effective marketing channels, they were able to promote their brand and attract customers without overspending.

Managing employee-related costs was another area where Michael and Clara exercised prudence. They offered competitive salaries and benefits to attract and retain talented employees but also implemented performance-based incentives to align employee goals with business objectives. By fostering a positive work environment and encouraging high performance, they maximized the value they got from their workforce.

To further control expenses, Michael and Clara regularly reviewed their business expenses for any unnecessary or redundant costs. They scrutinized every expense, from office supplies to subscriptions and memberships, to ensure that each expenditure was necessary and provided value to the business. This practice of regular expense audits helped them eliminate waste and make more informed spending decisions.

Another key aspect of expense management was leveraging technology to improve efficiency and reduce costs. Michael and

Clara adopted cloud-based accounting software that automated many accounting tasks, reducing the time and effort required for manual bookkeeping. They also used project management tools to streamline their operations and improve collaboration among their team. By embracing technology, they were able to operate more efficiently and keep costs under control.

Cash flow management was an integral part of their expense management strategy. Michael and Clara closely monitored their cash flow to ensure they had sufficient liquidity to meet their obligations. They implemented policies for timely invoicing and followed up promptly on overdue accounts receivable. By maintaining a healthy cash flow, they were able to avoid costly short-term borrowing and maintain financial stability.

Michael and Clara also understood the importance of planning for unexpected expenses. They established an emergency fund to cover any unforeseen costs, such as equipment repairs or sudden drops in sales. This financial cushion provided them with peace of mind and allowed them to navigate challenges without jeopardizing their business.

As Artisan Coffee Roasters continued to grow, Michael and Clara remained committed to controlling costs effectively. They recognized that expense management was not a one-time effort but an ongoing process that required vigilance and adaptability. They regularly revisited their expense management strategies, staying informed about industry trends and best practices to ensure they were always optimizing their cost structure.

Determining the value of a company's assets is a crucial task that can significantly impact financial reporting, decision-making, and strategic planning. Asset valuation involves assessing the worth of a company's assets, which can include everything from physical property and equipment to intangible assets like patents and trademarks. Accurate asset valuation ensures that a business's financial statements reflect true economic value, providing stakeholders with reliable information. The journey of Sarah, a small business owner of a boutique software development firm, provides a practical framework for understanding various asset valuation methods and their applications.

Sarah's firm, TechSolutions, started small but quickly grew, developing custom software solutions for a diverse range of clients. As the company expanded, Sarah realized the importance of understanding the value of her firm's assets to make informed business decisions, secure financing, and plan for future growth. She embarked on a comprehensive exploration of asset valuation methods, each tailored to different types of assets and business needs.

One of the first methods Sarah encountered was the **cost approach**. This method involves determining the value of an asset based on its historical cost, adjusted for depreciation. For tangible assets like office buildings, computer equipment, and office furniture, the cost approach provided a straightforward way to estimate their current value. Sarah meticulously tracked the purchase prices of these assets and applied standard depreciation methods to account for their wear and tear over time. This approach gave her a clear picture of the book value of her tangible assets, which was essential for financial reporting and tax purposes.

However, Sarah soon realized that the cost approach had limitations, especially for assets that could appreciate in value or for those that had unique characteristics. For example, the value of her office building in a rapidly developing tech hub was likely higher than its depreciated book value. To address this, she turned to the **market approach**, which estimates an asset's value based on the prices of similar assets in the market. By researching recent sales of comparable office properties in her area, Sarah was able to estimate a more accurate current market value for her building. This approach was particularly useful when she needed to provide collateral for a business loan, as it reflected the asset's true potential value in the current market conditions.

When it came to valuing TechSolutions' intangible assets, such as proprietary software and intellectual property, Sarah found the **income approach** to be highly effective. This method estimates the value of an asset based on the present value of the future income it is expected to generate. Sarah projected the future cash flows from her company's flagship software products, considering factors like market demand, competition, and technological advancements. She then discounted these future cash flows to their present value using an appropriate discount rate, reflecting the risk associated with the software market. The income approach allowed Sarah to capture the economic value of her intangible assets, which was crucial for attracting investors and negotiating licensing agreements.

For a more holistic view of her company's asset value, Sarah combined these primary valuation methods with additional techniques tailored to specific circumstances. For instance, when assessing the value of a potential acquisition target, she used the **comparative company analysis (CCA)** method. This involved comparing the financial metrics of the target company with those of similar companies in the industry. By examining multiples such as price-to-earnings (P/E) and enterprise value-to-sales (EV/S), Sarah could estimate a reasonable acquisition price that aligned with market standards.

Another valuable method Sarah explored was the **replacement cost approach**, particularly useful for insurance purposes. This method estimates the cost to replace an asset with a new one of similar functionality. For her computer servers and specialized software development tools, Sarah calculated the cost of acquiring equivalent new equipment and software. This approach ensured that her insurance coverage was adequate to replace essential assets in the event of damage or loss, providing peace of mind and financial security for her business.

As Sarah delved deeper into asset valuation, she recognized the importance of consistency and rigor in applying these methods. She established a systematic process for regular asset valuation reviews, ensuring that her financial statements remained accurate and up-to-date. By maintaining detailed records of asset purchases, market research, and valuation calculations, Sarah created a robust documentation trail that could withstand scrutiny from auditors, investors, and regulators.

Moreover, Sarah understood that the choice of valuation method could significantly impact her business's financial health and strategic decisions. For example, overvaluing assets could lead to inflated financial statements and unrealistic growth expectations, while undervaluing assets might result in missed opportunities for financing and investment. To navigate these challenges, she sought the advice of professional appraisers and valuation experts, whose insights and expertise helped her refine her valuation techniques and achieve more accurate results.

Through her journey of mastering asset valuation, Sarah also learned the value of transparency and communication with stakeholders. She shared her valuation methodologies and assumptions with her management team, investors, and financial partners, fostering a culture of openness and trust. This transparency not only built confidence in TechSolutions' financial integrity but also facilitated informed decision-making and strategic planning across the organization.

In addition to the technical aspects of asset valuation, Sarah appreciated the broader strategic implications. Accurate asset valuation enabled her to make informed decisions about resource allocation, investments, and growth opportunities. For instance, knowing the true value of her company's proprietary software allowed her to negotiate better licensing deals and partnerships. It also helped her prioritize which projects to invest in, ensuring that the company's resources were directed towards the most valuable and profitable ventures.

3.4. Depreciation Strategies: Maximizing Value

Depreciation is an essential concept in accounting and finance, representing the gradual reduction in the value of an asset over its useful life. Understanding and implementing effective depreciation strategies can significantly influence a company's financial health, tax liabilities, and overall asset management. This chapter delves into the various methods of depreciation, exploring their applications, benefits, and implications for maximizing value within a business.

Jane, a seasoned financial manager at a mid-sized manufacturing firm, knew that effectively managing depreciation was vital for her company's financial success. With a considerable investment in machinery, vehicles, and other fixed assets, Jane's goal was to optimize the company's depreciation strategy to enhance cash flow, reduce tax liabilities, and ensure accurate financial reporting.

One of the most straightforward methods Jane employed was the **straight-line depreciation** method. This approach spreads the cost of an asset evenly over its useful life. For instance, if a piece of machinery worth $100,000 had a useful life of ten years, Jane would allocate $10,000 annually as depreciation expense. The simplicity and predictability of straight-line depreciation made it an attractive option for financial reporting and budgeting, providing a clear and consistent picture of asset value reduction over time.

However, Jane also recognized the limitations of the straight-line method, particularly for assets that lost value more quickly in the initial years of use. To address this, she considered the **declining balance method**, which accelerates depreciation early in an asset's life. Using this method, a higher depreciation expense is recorded in the earlier years, reflecting the rapid decrease in the asset's value. For example, applying a 20% declining balance rate to the same $100,000 machinery would result in a $20,000 depreciation expense in the first year, $16,000 in the second year, and so on. This approach was especially beneficial for tax purposes, as it allowed Jane's company to defer taxes by claiming higher depreciation expenses upfront, thereby enhancing immediate cash flow.

In addition to the declining balance method, Jane explored the **double-declining balance method**, an even more accelerated form of depreciation. This method doubled the straight-line depreciation rate, providing an aggressive depreciation schedule that could significantly reduce taxable income in the initial years of an asset's life. For the $100,000 machinery with a ten-year useful life, the double-declining balance method would result in a $20,000 depreciation expense in the first year, $16,000 in the second year, and so forth. While this method increased complexity in calculations, the substantial early tax benefits made it a valuable strategy for managing cash flow and reinvesting in business growth.

Jane also considered the **units of production method**, which based depreciation on an asset's usage rather than time. For assets like manufacturing equipment that experienced variable usage, this method provided a more accurate reflection of wear and tear. By estimating the total production capacity of the machinery and allocating depreciation based on actual usage, Jane ensured that the depreciation expense matched the asset's operational reality. For instance, if the $100,000 machinery was expected to produce 1 million units over its useful life, and it produced 100,000 units in the first year, the depreciation expense for that year would be $10,000. This method allowed Jane to align depreciation with production levels, offering a realistic portrayal of asset value reduction.

Beyond selecting the appropriate depreciation method, Jane understood the importance of **regularly reviewing and updating** depreciation schedules. Changes in asset usage, market conditions, and technological advancements could impact the useful life and residual value of assets. By conducting annual reviews and adjusting depreciation estimates as needed, Jane ensured that her company's financial statements remained accurate and reflective of current asset values. This proactive approach also helped identify underperforming or obsolete assets, enabling timely decisions on repairs, upgrades, or disposals.

Jane's strategic approach to depreciation extended to her **tax planning** efforts. She leveraged tax incentives and allowances, such as bonus depreciation and Section 179 expensing, to maximize tax benefits. Bonus depreciation allowed Jane to immediately deduct a significant portion of the asset's cost in the year of purchase, while Section 179 expensing provided an opportunity to expense the full cost of qualifying assets up to a certain limit. By combining these tax benefits with her chosen depreciation methods, Jane effectively reduced her company's taxable income, freeing up resources for reinvestment and growth.

Moreover, Jane's comprehensive depreciation strategy played a crucial role in **financial planning and decision-making**. Accurate depreciation schedules provided valuable insights into the true cost of asset ownership, including maintenance, operating expenses, and eventual replacement costs. This information was vital for budgeting, forecasting, and evaluating the return on investment for new capital expenditures. By understanding the full financial impact of asset acquisitions and disposals, Jane could make informed decisions that aligned with her company's long-term strategic goals.

Jane's experience highlights several key takeaways for effectively managing depreciation and maximizing value:

Choose the Right Method: Select a depreciation method that aligns with the asset's usage patterns and the company's financial objectives. Consider the benefits and limitations of each method, such as straight-line, declining balance, double-declining balance, and units of production, to determine which best suits your business needs.

Leverage Tax Benefits: Utilize tax incentives and allowances like bonus depreciation and Section 179 expensing to maximize tax savings. These provisions can significantly impact cash flow and provide immediate financial benefits that can be reinvested into the business.

Regularly Review and Update: Conduct annual reviews of asset depreciation schedules to ensure they reflect current usage, market conditions, and technological advancements. Adjust estimates as necessary to maintain accurate financial reporting and asset management.

Integrate Depreciation into Financial Planning: Use depreciation data to inform budgeting, forecasting, and capital expenditure decisions. Understanding the full financial impact of asset ownership helps in making strategic decisions that support long-term business goals.

Document and Justify: Maintain detailed records of your depreciation methods, calculations, and rationale. This documentation is crucial for audit trails, financial transparency, and compliance with accounting standards and tax regulations.

Educate and Communicate: Ensure that your financial team understands the chosen depreciation strategies and their implications. Clear communication about depreciation's impact on financial statements and tax liabilities fosters better decision-making and alignment across the organization.

Jane's approach also emphasized the importance of strategic asset management. By closely monitoring the depreciation of her assets, she could identify when equipment was nearing the end of its useful life and plan for replacements or upgrades accordingly. This proactive asset management prevented unexpected breakdowns and production halts, ensuring continuous operational efficiency and productivity.

One particularly insightful instance in Jane's career was when her company decided to invest in a new production line. The initial cost was substantial, and the financial implications of this investment were significant. Jane applied a combination of straight-line and units of production depreciation methods to this new line. The straight-line approach provided a predictable annual expense for financial reporting, while the units of production method allowed for more accurate expense allocation based on actual usage. This dual-method approach gave a clearer financial picture, balancing simplicity in reporting with precision in cost management.

Jane's expertise also extended to the disposal of assets. She meticulously tracked the net book value of assets set for disposal, ensuring that any gains or losses were accurately recorded. This attention to detail minimized the risk of financial discrepancies and provided a clearer understanding of the company's capital gains or losses, crucial for both tax purposes and internal financial analysis.

Another best practice Jane implemented was the use of depreciation software. These tools automated much of the depreciation calculation process, reducing the risk of human error and increasing efficiency. The software also facilitated scenario analysis, allowing Jane to model the financial impact of different depreciation strategies before implementation. This capability was particularly useful during strategic planning sessions and when presenting options to the executive team.

In her role, Jane also emphasized the importance of compliance with accounting standards and regulations. She ensured that her company's depreciation methods adhered to Generally Accepted Accounting Principles (GAAP) and International Financial Reporting Standards (IFRS). Compliance not only avoided legal and financial penalties but also built trust with investors, auditors, and other stakeholders.

Jane's comprehensive approach to depreciation management was not without challenges. She often had to balance the financial benefits of accelerated depreciation methods with the need for accurate and transparent reporting. Additionally, changes in tax laws and accounting standards required continuous learning and adaptation. However, her commitment to ongoing education and staying abreast of industry developments enabled her to navigate these challenges effectively.

By sharing her knowledge and experiences, Jane also mentored junior accountants and financial analysts in her company. She conducted training sessions on the various depreciation methods, tax implications, and the importance of accurate asset management. This knowledge transfer not only built a more capable finance team but also ensured that the company's depreciation strategies were consistently applied and understood across the organization.

Jane's story provides a clear roadmap for effectively managing depreciation to maximize value. Her strategic use of different depreciation methods, leveraging tax benefits, regular reviews, and integration with financial planning underscores the importance of a holistic approach to asset management. By applying these principles, businesses can optimize their financial performance, enhance cash flow, and make informed decisions that drive long-term success.

Ultimately, the goal of any depreciation strategy should be to reflect the true economic value of assets accurately while supporting the company's broader financial and strategic objectives. Whether it's through straightforward methods like straight-line depreciation or more complex approaches like units of production, the key lies in understanding the unique needs of the business and aligning depreciation practices accordingly.

Jane's meticulous approach serves as a powerful example of how effective depreciation management can contribute to a company's financial health and operational success. By adopting similar strategies, business leaders can ensure that their asset management practices not only comply with accounting standards and tax regulations but also support sustainable growth and profitability.

3.5. Liability Management: Balancing Debt and Equity

Balancing debt and equity is a critical component of effective liability management, a task that requires both strategic insight and financial acumen. For businesses seeking to optimize their capital structure, understanding the intricate dance between debt and equity is essential. This chapter explores the nuances of liability management, offering practical advice to beginners on how to balance these two elements to support sustainable growth and financial stability.

Sarah, the CFO of a rapidly growing tech startup, faced the challenge of financing her company's expansion without compromising its financial health. She knew that a well-balanced mix of debt and equity could provide the necessary funds while maintaining flexibility and minimizing risk. Her journey offers valuable insights into the principles and practices of effective liability management.

Debt, often seen as a double-edged sword, can provide immediate capital needed for growth, but it also comes with the obligation to repay with interest. Sarah understood that leveraging debt could amplify her company's returns, especially during periods of high growth. However, she was equally aware of the risks associated with excessive borrowing, including the potential for financial distress and the burden of regular interest payments.

To navigate this complexity, Sarah first assessed her company's current financial position, examining key metrics such as the debt-to-equity ratio, interest coverage ratio, and current ratio.

These metrics provided a clear picture of her company's ability to meet its short-term obligations and its overall financial leverage. A debt-to-equity ratio of 1:1, for instance, indicated that her company had equal parts debt and equity, while a higher ratio suggested greater reliance on debt.

Armed with this information, Sarah began exploring different debt instruments that could fit her company's needs. She considered traditional bank loans, which offered fixed interest rates and predictable repayment schedules, providing stability and ease of planning. However, she also took into account the stringent covenants often attached to these loans, which could restrict her company's operational flexibility.

Sarah then looked into issuing corporate bonds as an alternative. Bonds could raise substantial capital without diluting ownership, a key consideration for her startup. By offering bonds with varying maturities and interest rates, she could attract a diverse group of investors while managing the overall cost of capital. However, she also recognized the need to maintain a strong credit rating, as any downgrade could increase borrowing costs and limit access to future capital.

In parallel with her debt strategy, Sarah evaluated equity financing options. Issuing new shares could provide the necessary funds without the immediate pressure of repayment. This approach was particularly attractive given her company's high growth potential, which promised substantial returns for investors. Yet, she was mindful of the downside—dilution of existing shareholders' equity and potential loss of control over strategic decisions.

To strike the right balance, Sarah decided to adopt a hybrid approach, combining debt and equity financing. She opted for a moderate level of debt to take advantage of the tax deductibility of interest payments while issuing new shares to maintain liquidity and support long-term growth. This strategy allowed her to leverage the benefits of both financing methods while mitigating their respective risks.

One practical example of Sarah's approach was the decision to finance the development of a new product line. She secured a bank loan with favorable terms, using the predictable revenue from the existing product portfolio to service the debt. Simultaneously, she conducted a secondary offering of shares to raise additional equity capital, ensuring that the company had sufficient funds to cover unforeseen expenses and invest in marketing and distribution.

Effective liability management also required Sarah to maintain a keen eye on market conditions and economic trends. She closely monitored interest rates, inflation, and investor sentiment, adjusting her strategy as needed. For instance, during periods of low interest rates, she favored longer-term debt to lock in favorable borrowing costs. Conversely, when equity markets were buoyant, she capitalized on high valuations to issue new shares at attractive prices.

Beyond financial metrics and market conditions, Sarah also prioritized maintaining a strong relationship with her company's investors and lenders. Transparent communication and regular updates on the company's performance and strategic direction helped build trust and confidence. This goodwill proved invaluable during challenging times, providing her company with the flexibility and support needed to navigate financial uncertainties.

Sarah's approach to liability management also included a robust risk management framework. She implemented hedging strategies to protect against interest rate fluctuations and currency risks, ensuring that her company's financial position remained stable. Additionally, she maintained a contingency plan with access to emergency lines of credit, ready to be deployed in case of unexpected cash flow disruptions.

Another critical aspect of Sarah's strategy was the regular review and adjustment of her company's capital structure. She scheduled quarterly reviews to assess the effectiveness of her financing mix, making necessary adjustments to align with the company's evolving needs and market conditions. This proactive approach allowed her to stay ahead of potential issues and capitalize on new opportunities as they arose.

Sarah's journey underscores the importance of a balanced and dynamic approach to liability management. By carefully assessing her company's financial position, exploring various financing options, and maintaining flexibility, she successfully balanced debt and equity to support sustainable growth. Her story provides a practical roadmap for beginners looking to navigate the complexities of liability management and optimize their capital structure.

In conclusion, effective liability management is a dynamic process that requires continuous assessment, strategic decision-making, and adaptability. Balancing debt and equity is not a one-time task but an ongoing effort to align a company's financing needs with its growth objectives and market conditions. By understanding the interplay between debt and equity, businesses can create a resilient financial structure that supports their long-term goals.

Chapter 4: Strategic Decision-Making with Financial Data

4.1. Financial Statement Analysis: Ratios and Metrics

Understanding financial statement analysis through ratios and metrics is akin to learning a new language, one that speaks volumes about a company's health, performance, and potential. For beginners, deciphering these numbers might seem daunting, but with a structured approach, it becomes a powerful tool for making informed decisions. This chapter delves into the key ratios and metrics that form the backbone of financial analysis, offering practical insights and actionable advice.

Imagine you're an investor scrutinizing a potential company's financial statements. You'd want to know if the company is profitable, how efficiently it uses its resources, and whether it has a sound financial footing. This is where financial ratios come into play. Ratios distill complex financial data into simple, comparable numbers, making it easier to gauge the company's performance relative to its peers or its historical performance.

One of the most fundamental areas of financial analysis is profitability. Profitability ratios help assess a company's ability to generate earnings relative to its revenue, assets, equity, and other metrics. The gross profit margin, for instance, tells you how much of each dollar of revenue is left after accounting for the cost of goods sold. A higher margin indicates efficient production and pricing strategies. To calculate it, divide gross profit by revenue.

Next, the operating profit margin, also known as EBIT (Earnings Before Interest and Taxes) margin, measures the percentage of revenue left after covering operating expenses but before paying interest and taxes. This ratio provides insight into the company's operational efficiency. A high operating margin can suggest strong control over operating costs. Calculate it by dividing EBIT by revenue.

Net profit margin goes a step further, showing the percentage of revenue that remains as profit after all expenses, including taxes and interest, are deducted. This is a comprehensive measure of overall profitability. To find it, divide net income by revenue. A consistently high net profit margin indicates robust financial health and profitability.

Beyond profitability, efficiency ratios shed light on how well a company utilizes its assets and liabilities. The inventory turnover ratio, for example, reveals how often a company's inventory is sold and replaced over a period. A higher ratio indicates efficient inventory management. Calculate it by dividing the cost of goods sold by average inventory. Conversely, a low turnover might suggest overstocking or obsolescence issues.

The accounts receivable turnover ratio measures how effectively a company collects on its receivables. A higher ratio implies efficient credit practices and swift collection. To calculate it, divide net credit sales by average accounts receivable. Monitoring this ratio helps in understanding the liquidity and operational efficiency of a company.

Asset turnover ratio is another critical metric, indicating how efficiently a company uses its assets to generate sales. A higher ratio suggests better asset utilization. Calculate it by dividing net sales by average total assets. This ratio is particularly useful for comparing companies within the same industry.

Liquidity ratios are essential for assessing a company's ability to meet its short-term obligations. The current ratio, one of the most well-known liquidity metrics, compares current assets to current liabilities. A ratio above 1 indicates that the company has more current assets than current liabilities, suggesting good short-term financial health. Calculate it by dividing current assets by current liabilities.

The quick ratio, or acid-test ratio, is a more stringent measure of liquidity, excluding inventory from current assets. It assesses whether a company can meet its short-term obligations without selling inventory. A quick ratio of 1 or higher is generally considered healthy. Calculate it by subtracting inventory from current assets and then dividing the result by current liabilities.

Solvency ratios, on the other hand, evaluate a company's long-term financial stability and its ability to meet long-term obligations. The debt-to-equity ratio compares total debt to total equity, providing insight into the company's financial leverage. A lower ratio suggests a more financially stable company with less reliance on debt. Calculate it by dividing total liabilities by total shareholders' equity.

The interest coverage ratio measures a company's ability to pay interest on its outstanding debt. A higher ratio indicates greater ease in covering interest expenses, reflecting financial health and stability. Calculate it by dividing EBIT by interest expense.

Return on assets (ROA) and return on equity (ROE) are crucial for understanding the returns generated on investments in the company. ROA measures how efficiently a company uses its assets to generate profit, calculated by dividing net income by average total assets. ROE, on the other hand, assesses the return generated on shareholders' equity, calculated by dividing net income by average shareholders' equity. High ROA and ROE values typically indicate effective management and strong financial performance.

While ratios and metrics provide invaluable insights, they are most effective when used in context. Comparing ratios against industry benchmarks, historical performance, and competitor data can reveal trends and outliers that might not be apparent in isolation. For instance, a high debt-to-equity ratio might be typical in capital-intensive industries but alarming in others.

Let's consider a practical example. Jane, a budding investor, is evaluating two companies in the retail sector. By examining their financial statements, she calculates the following ratios for each company:

Company   A:
Gross Profit Margin: 40%

Operating Profit Margin: 15%

Net Profit Margin: 10%

Inventory Turnover Ratio: 5 times

Accounts Receivable Turnover Ratio: 8 times

Asset Turnover Ratio: 1.5 times

Current Ratio: 2.0

Quick Ratio: 1.5

Debt-to-Equity Ratio: 0.5

Interest Coverage Ratio: 10 times

ROA: 12%

ROE: 18%

Company B:

Gross Profit Margin: 35%

Operating Profit Margin: 12%

Net Profit Margin: 8%

Inventory Turnover Ratio: 6 times

Accounts Receivable Turnover Ratio: 7 times

Asset Turnover Ratio: 1.2 times

Current Ratio: 1.8

Quick Ratio: 1.2

Debt-to-Equity Ratio: 0.7

Interest Coverage Ratio: 8 times

ROA: 10%

ROE: 15%

By analyzing these ratios, Jane can draw several conclusions. Company A demonstrates higher profitability across all margins, suggesting better cost management and pricing strategies. Its lower inventory turnover ratio compared to Company B indicates it might be holding onto inventory longer, which could be a concern if inventory becomes obsolete, but this is offset by a high accounts receivable turnover ratio, indicating efficient collection practices.

In terms of liquidity, both companies appear healthy, but Company A's higher current and quick ratios suggest it is better positioned to meet short-term obligations. The lower debt-to-equity ratio for Company A indicates a more conservative use of debt, reducing financial risk. Additionally, Company A's higher interest coverage ratio implies it can comfortably meet its interest obligations, further reflecting financial stability.

When it comes to asset efficiency, Company B has a higher inventory turnover ratio, which means it's selling and replacing its inventory more frequently than Company A. However, Company A's higher asset turnover ratio suggests it is generating more revenue per dollar of assets, indicating overall better asset utilization.

Company A also outperforms in return metrics, with higher ROA and ROE, signifying more effective use of assets and equity to generate profits. These figures suggest that Company A is more efficient in converting its investments into net income.

However, ratios should not be looked at in isolation. Jane should also consider qualitative factors such as market position, management quality, competitive landscape, and economic conditions. For instance, if Company A operates in a more stable market or has a stronger brand presence, this could further justify its superior financial metrics.

Another practical approach involves using financial ratios to monitor a company's performance over time. For example, if Jane notices that Company A's debt-to-equity ratio has been rising steadily while its interest coverage ratio is declining, this could signal increasing financial risk, prompting a deeper investigation into its debt management strategies.

Similarly, a declining net profit margin might indicate rising costs or pricing pressures, necessitating a review of the company's cost control measures and competitive environment. Tracking these trends helps in identifying potential issues early, allowing for timely corrective actions.

To effectively utilize financial ratios, beginners should develop a systematic approach to financial statement analysis. Start by gathering all necessary financial statements, including the balance sheet, income statement, and cash flow statement.

Ensure the data is accurate and up-to-date. Then, calculate the relevant ratios, comparing them against industry benchmarks and historical data.

It's also beneficial to use visualization tools like graphs and charts to track these ratios over time. Visual representations can make it easier to spot trends and anomalies, facilitating more intuitive analysis.

Moreover, integrating financial ratios into a broader analysis framework can enhance decision-making. For instance, combining ratio analysis with SWOT (Strengths, Weaknesses, Opportunities, Threats) analysis provides a more comprehensive view of a company's financial health and strategic positioning.

In conclusion, financial statement analysis through ratios and metrics is a vital skill for anyone looking to understand a company's financial performance and make informed investment or management decisions. By mastering these tools, you can demystify complex financial data, uncovering insights that drive strategic actions. Remember to always consider the context, use multiple ratios for a well-rounded view, and stay vigilant for trends over time. With practice and diligence, financial ratios become not just numbers but powerful indicators of potential and performance.

4.2. Budgeting and Forecasting: Planning for the Future

Every successful business journey involves meticulous planning and foresight. Budgeting and forecasting are critical tools that help organizations chart a course toward their financial goals and navigate the uncertainties of the future. By creating detailed budgets and accurate forecasts, businesses can allocate resources efficiently, anticipate challenges, and capitalize on opportunities.

Consider the story of Emma, a young entrepreneur who founded a small tech startup. When Emma launched her business, she quickly realized the importance of budgeting and forecasting. Without them, she was steering her company blindfolded, unable to anticipate cash flow needs or plan for growth. By implementing robust budgeting and forecasting practices, Emma transformed her startup into a thriving enterprise.

Budgeting is the process of creating a detailed financial plan for a specific period, usually a year. It involves projecting revenues and expenses, setting financial targets, and allocating resources accordingly. A well-crafted budget serves as a roadmap, guiding a company's financial decisions and ensuring alignment with its strategic goals.

Start by analyzing historical financial data. This provides a solid foundation for making informed projections. Look at past revenues, costs, and seasonality trends. Historical data helps identify patterns and variances that are crucial for accurate budgeting. For Emma, examining her startup's first-year performance revealed that sales spiked during the holiday season, prompting her to allocate more marketing funds for that period.

Next, involve key stakeholders in the budgeting process. Collaboration ensures that the budget reflects realistic expectations and aligns with departmental goals. Emma engaged her sales, marketing, and operations teams to gather input and set achievable targets. This collaborative approach fostered accountability and buy-in from all departments.

Revenue projections are a critical component of the budget. They should be based on realistic assumptions, considering market conditions, competitive landscape, and internal capabilities. Overly optimistic projections can lead to resource shortages and missed targets. Emma used a conservative approach, incorporating different scenarios to account for uncertainties.

Expense planning is equally important. Categorize expenses into fixed and variable costs. Fixed costs, such as rent and salaries, remain constant regardless of business activity. Variable costs, such as raw materials and shipping, fluctuate with sales volume. Identifying these costs helps in understanding the financial impact of different business activities.

Emma also established a contingency fund within her budget. This reserve covered unexpected expenses and emergencies, such as equipment breakdowns or sudden market shifts. Having a contingency fund provided a safety net, ensuring that her startup could navigate unforeseen challenges without derailing its financial stability.

Once the budget is finalized, it's crucial to monitor and adjust it regularly. Financial performance should be tracked against the budget to identify variances. Significant deviations necessitate a review and potential adjustments. Emma reviewed her budget quarterly, adjusting her plans based on actual performance and changing market conditions. This iterative process kept her financial plans relevant and responsive.

Forecasting, on the other hand, involves predicting future financial outcomes based on current data and trends. While budgeting is a static plan, forecasting is dynamic and adaptable, providing ongoing insights into future performance. Accurate forecasting enables proactive decision-making and strategic planning.

Emma used various forecasting methods to predict her startup's future performance. One common approach is trend analysis, which examines historical data to identify patterns and project future results. For instance, if sales have consistently grown by 10% annually, trend analysis can help forecast similar growth in the coming year.

Regression analysis is another powerful tool. It examines the relationship between different variables to predict future outcomes. Emma used regression analysis to understand how factors like marketing spend and customer acquisition costs influenced sales. This allowed her to make data-driven decisions about resource allocation.

Scenario analysis is particularly useful for dealing with uncertainties. It involves creating multiple forecasts based on different assumptions and scenarios. For example, Emma developed best-case, worst-case, and most-likely scenarios for her startup's sales. This approach helped her prepare for various outcomes and devise contingency plans.

Rolling forecasts are an effective way to keep projections up-to-date. Unlike static annual budgets, rolling forecasts are updated regularly, usually monthly or quarterly, to reflect the latest data and trends. Emma adopted rolling forecasts for her cash flow projections, ensuring that her financial plans remained relevant and accurate throughout the year.

Cash flow forecasting is critical for maintaining liquidity and ensuring that a business can meet its obligations. It involves projecting cash inflows and outflows to anticipate periods of surplus or shortfall. Emma created a detailed cash flow forecast, tracking expected cash receipts from sales and planned payments for expenses. This enabled her to manage working capital effectively and avoid cash crunches.

Integrating budgeting and forecasting enhances financial planning and performance management. Emma used her budget as a baseline and her forecasts to track progress and make adjustments. This integrated approach provided a comprehensive view of her startup's financial health and future prospects.

Technology plays a vital role in modern budgeting and forecasting. Financial software and tools can automate data collection, analysis, and reporting, making the process more efficient and accurate. Emma leveraged cloud-based financial software to streamline her budgeting and forecasting activities, freeing up time for strategic decision-making.

Effective budgeting and forecasting require a combination of analytical skills, strategic thinking, and collaboration. Emma cultivated a culture of financial discipline within her startup, ensuring that all team members understood the importance of these practices and contributed to them. She held regular training sessions to improve her team's financial literacy and encouraged open communication about financial matters.

4.3. Cost-Benefit Analysis: Making Informed Decisions

Imagine you're at the helm of a growing business, faced with myriad decisions each day. Some choices are straightforward, while others carry significant financial implications that could shape the future of your enterprise. This is where cost-benefit analysis (CBA) becomes an invaluable tool, enabling you to make informed decisions by systematically weighing the costs and benefits of various options.

Cost-benefit analysis is a structured approach to evaluating the potential impacts of a decision. It involves identifying, quantifying, and comparing the costs and benefits associated with a particular course of action. This method helps ensure that resources are allocated efficiently and that the potential returns justify the investment.

Consider the story of Jake, who runs a small manufacturing company. Jake was contemplating whether to invest in a new piece of machinery that promised to increase production efficiency. The machine came with a hefty price tag, and Jake needed to determine if the investment would pay off in the long run. By conducting a thorough cost-benefit analysis, he could make a well-informed decision.

The first step in conducting a CBA is to identify all the relevant costs and benefits. Costs can be direct, such as the purchase price of equipment, or indirect, like the training expenses for staff to use the new machinery. Benefits might include increased production, reduced labor costs, and improved product quality. Jake began by listing all the potential costs, including the price of the machine, installation fees, maintenance costs, and any potential downtime during the transition period. He also identified the benefits, such as increased output, lower per-unit production costs, and the potential for higher sales.

Quantifying these costs and benefits is crucial. This often involves assigning monetary values to both tangible and intangible factors. Direct costs are typically easier to quantify, but indirect costs and benefits, such as employee satisfaction or customer perception, can be more challenging. Jake worked with his financial team to estimate the monetary value of the increased production and the savings from reduced labor costs. They also considered the potential revenue from entering new markets with the improved efficiency of their production process.

Next, Jake needed to compare the total costs and benefits over a relevant time period. This is where the concept of present value comes into play. Future costs and benefits must be discounted to their present value to account for the time value of money. Jake's financial team used a discount rate to calculate the present value of the expected benefits and compared it to the present value of the costs. This step allowed them to determine the net present value (NPV) of the investment.

A positive NPV indicates that the benefits outweigh the costs, making the investment worthwhile. Conversely, a negative NPV suggests that the costs exceed the benefits, and the investment should be reconsidered. Jake's analysis revealed a positive NPV, suggesting that purchasing the new machinery would indeed be a beneficial investment for his company.

Sensitivity analysis is another critical component of CBA. It involves testing the robustness of the results by varying key assumptions and parameters. This helps identify which factors have the most significant impact on the outcome and assess the risk associated with the decision. Jake conducted a sensitivity analysis to see how changes in production volume, maintenance costs, and discount rates would affect the NPV. This exercise provided him with a range of possible outcomes and highlighted the variables that required close monitoring.

While cost-benefit analysis is a powerful tool, it is not without limitations. One challenge is accurately quantifying intangible benefits, such as improved employee morale or brand reputation. These factors can significantly impact a business but are often difficult to measure in monetary terms. Moreover, CBA can sometimes oversimplify complex decisions by focusing solely on quantifiable factors, potentially overlooking qualitative aspects that are equally important.

Despite these limitations, cost-benefit analysis remains a valuable framework for decision-making. By providing a systematic approach to evaluating the financial implications of various options, it helps ensure that resources are used effectively and that decisions are aligned with strategic goals.

For beginners looking to implement CBA in their decision-making process, it's essential to start with a clear understanding of the specific decision at hand and the context in which it is being made. Begin by gathering all relevant data and engaging with stakeholders who can provide insights into potential costs and benefits. This collaborative approach helps ensure that the analysis is comprehensive and considers multiple perspectives.

It's also important to maintain transparency throughout the process. Clearly document all assumptions, methodologies, and calculations used in the analysis. This not only facilitates better understanding and communication but also allows for easier review and adjustment if necessary.

Consider the case of Sarah, who managed a retail chain. She faced a decision about whether to launch an e-commerce platform to complement her brick-and-mortar stores. Sarah's team conducted a CBA, identifying costs such as website development, digital marketing, and fulfillment logistics. The benefits included increased sales reach, convenience for customers, and potential market expansion. By carefully quantifying these factors and performing a sensitivity analysis, Sarah was able to make a data-driven decision that ultimately led to significant growth for her business.

Incorporating CBA into your decision-making toolkit can lead to more rational and justifiable choices. It equips you with a structured method to assess potential investments, projects, and strategies, ensuring that each decision is backed by thorough analysis and sound reasoning. Over time, this approach can significantly enhance your business's financial health and strategic positioning.

4.4. Investment Appraisal: Evaluating Opportunities

Investment appraisal is a critical process for any business, whether it's a startup seeking to expand or an established company looking to diversify. Evaluating opportunities effectively ensures that resources are allocated to projects that will yield the highest returns. This chapter delves into the intricacies of investment appraisal, providing actionable advice for beginners to make sound investment decisions.

Imagine you're Alex, the CEO of a mid-sized tech company. Your team has proposed several potential projects, from developing a new software product to expanding into international markets. Each option appears promising, but your resources are limited. How do you determine which project will deliver the best return on investment (ROI)? This is where investment appraisal techniques come into play.

The first step in investment appraisal is identifying the potential investments and understanding their scope. Alex's team came up with detailed proposals for each project, outlining the objectives, timeline, required resources, and expected outcomes. By clearly defining each opportunity, Alex ensured that every project could be evaluated on a comparable basis.

One of the most widely used methods for investment appraisal is the Net Present Value (NPV) analysis. NPV calculates the difference between the present value of cash inflows and the present value of cash outflows over a project's lifetime. A positive NPV indicates that the projected earnings (discounted to present value) exceed the anticipated costs, making the investment worthwhile.

Alex's financial team gathered data on the expected cash flows for each project. They estimated the revenues, operating costs, and initial investments required. Using an appropriate discount rate to account for the time value of money, they calculated the NPV for each project. Comparing these NPVs provided a clear picture of which projects were likely to be the most profitable.

Another essential technique is the Internal Rate of Return (IRR). The IRR is the discount rate that makes the NPV of an investment zero. In simpler terms, it's the expected annualized return of the project. Alex used IRR to determine the efficiency of each investment. Projects with an IRR higher than the company's cost of capital were considered favorable, as they promised returns greater than the minimum acceptable rate.

Payback period analysis is also a useful tool, especially for businesses that prioritize liquidity and risk management. This method calculates the time it takes for an investment to generate enough cash flow to recover the initial investment. Although it doesn't account for the time value of money or cash flows beyond the payback period, it provides a quick assessment of a project's risk. Alex's team calculated the payback periods for each project, helping them understand how quickly they could expect to recoup their investments.

Profitability Index (PI), also known as the benefit-cost ratio, is another valuable metric. It is calculated by dividing the present value of future cash flows by the initial investment. A PI greater than 1 indicates that the project is expected to generate more value than it costs. Alex used the PI to rank the projects, providing a straightforward comparison of their relative profitability.

While quantitative techniques are crucial, qualitative factors should not be overlooked. These include strategic alignment, market conditions, regulatory environment, and potential risks. For instance, Alex considered how each project aligned with the company's long-term goals and core competencies. Expanding into international markets might offer high returns, but it also involves significant regulatory and cultural challenges. On the other hand, developing a new software product could leverage the company's existing expertise and customer base.

Sensitivity analysis is another essential aspect of investment appraisal. It involves testing how sensitive the NPV or IRR is to changes in key assumptions, such as sales volume, cost of materials, or discount rates. Alex conducted sensitivity analyses to understand the potential variability in project outcomes. This process highlighted the critical factors that could impact the success of each investment, allowing Alex to plan for contingencies.

Scenario analysis takes this a step further by evaluating how different scenarios, such as best-case, worst-case, and most-likely-case, affect the project's viability. This approach helped Alex's team anticipate a range of possible outcomes and prepare for uncertainties. For example, they considered how fluctuations in exchange rates might impact the profitability of international expansion or how technological advancements could affect the competitiveness of the new software product.

Risk assessment is also integral to the appraisal process. Identifying and mitigating risks can significantly influence the success of an investment. Alex's team performed a thorough risk assessment for each project, identifying potential risks and developing strategies to mitigate them. This included considering market risks, operational risks, financial risks, and compliance risks. By proactively addressing these challenges, Alex could make more informed decisions and enhance the likelihood of successful project implementation.

Communication and stakeholder involvement are crucial throughout the appraisal process. Alex ensured that all relevant departments, including finance, marketing, operations, and legal, were involved in the appraisal process. This collaborative approach provided a comprehensive view of each project's potential impacts and fostered buy-in from key stakeholders.

Once the appraisal process was complete, Alex prioritized the projects based on their NPVs, IRRs, payback periods, PIs, and qualitative assessments. This prioritization helped allocate resources to the most promising opportunities, ensuring that the company's investments were aligned with its strategic objectives and financial goals. Alex's decision-making was now backed by a thorough, data-driven analysis, significantly reducing the risk of pursuing less lucrative or overly risky ventures.

4.5. Risk Management: Identifying and Mitigating Financial Risks

Emily, the CFO of a mid-sized manufacturing company, faced a daunting challenge. With the company's rapid growth, the financial landscape was becoming increasingly complex, and the potential risks were multiplying. Her primary mission was to identify these financial risks and develop strategies to mitigate them effectively. This chapter delves into the practical steps Emily took, offering a roadmap for anyone looking to navigate the uncertain waters of financial risk management.

The first step Emily took was to conduct a comprehensive risk assessment. She knew that identifying potential financial risks was crucial. These risks can be broadly categorized into market risk, credit risk, liquidity risk, and operational risk. Market risk involves potential losses due to changes in market conditions, such as fluctuations in interest rates, exchange rates, and commodity prices. Credit risk arises from the possibility that customers or counterparties may default on their obligations. Liquidity risk pertains to the company's ability to meet its short-term financial obligations, while operational risk includes potential losses due to internal failures, such as process breakdowns or fraud.

To identify these risks, Emily leveraged both quantitative and qualitative methods. She reviewed historical financial data, analyzed market trends, and consulted with various departments within the company. For instance, the sales team provided insights into customer payment behaviors, which helped assess credit risk. The procurement team offered information on supply chain vulnerabilities, contributing to the understanding of operational risk. By gathering a comprehensive set of data, Emily ensured that no significant risk was overlooked.

Once the risks were identified, the next step was to evaluate their potential impact. Emily prioritized the risks based on their likelihood and the severity of their consequences. She used risk matrices and scenario analysis to visualize and quantify these risks. For example, she considered the potential impact of a sudden increase in raw material prices on the company's profit margins and cash flow. By assigning probabilities and financial impacts to each risk, Emily created a clear picture of the company's risk exposure.

With a prioritized list of risks, Emily moved on to developing mitigation strategies. One effective approach was diversification. By diversifying the company's customer base, suppliers, and product lines, Emily could reduce the impact of any single adverse event. For instance, if a major customer defaulted on their payments, the financial impact would be cushioned by revenues from other customers. Similarly, sourcing raw materials from multiple suppliers minimized the risk of supply chain disruptions.

Another key strategy was the use of financial instruments such as hedging. Hedging involves using derivatives like futures, options, and swaps to offset potential losses from adverse market movements. Emily's company, for example, entered into futures contracts to lock in the prices of key raw materials, thereby protecting against price volatility. Hedging could also be used to manage currency risk by locking in exchange rates for future transactions, ensuring that fluctuations in currency values did not erode profit margins.

Insurance was another vital tool in risk management. By purchasing insurance policies, Emily transferred specific risks to an insurance company. This included coverage for property damage, liability claims, business interruption, and more. While insurance did not eliminate the risk, it provided financial compensation in the event of a covered loss, thereby mitigating the financial impact on the company.

Strong internal controls and corporate governance were also essential components of risk management. Emily worked closely with the company's internal audit team to ensure that robust controls were in place to prevent and detect fraud, errors, and inefficiencies. This included implementing segregation of duties, regular financial audits, and comprehensive reporting mechanisms. By fostering a culture of transparency and accountability, Emily enhanced the company's ability to manage operational risks effectively.

Stress testing and scenario planning were critical for understanding how the company would perform under adverse conditions. Emily conducted regular stress tests to simulate the impact of various negative scenarios, such as a severe economic downturn, a natural disaster, or a major technological disruption. These tests helped identify potential weaknesses in the company's financial structure and provided valuable insights into how to strengthen resilience. For instance, stress testing might reveal that the company's cash reserves were insufficient to withstand a prolonged economic recession, prompting Emily to advocate for building a larger cash buffer.

Effective communication and stakeholder engagement were crucial throughout the risk management process. Emily ensured that senior management, the board of directors, and key employees were kept informed about the company's risk profile and mitigation strategies. Regular risk management reports and presentations helped maintain awareness and foster a proactive risk management culture. Additionally, involving stakeholders in the risk management process ensured that diverse perspectives were considered, leading to more comprehensive and robust risk mitigation plans.

Monitoring and reviewing the risk management framework was an ongoing task. Emily established key risk indicators (KRIs) to track the company's risk exposure and the effectiveness of mitigation strategies. These indicators were monitored regularly, and any significant changes in risk levels triggered a review of the corresponding mitigation plans. For example, if the KRI for credit risk showed an increase in customer payment defaults, Emily would investigate the underlying causes and adjust credit policies accordingly.

To illustrate how Emily's company implemented these risk management strategies, consider the following scenario. The company was heavily reliant on a single supplier for a critical raw material. Recently, there had been warnings of potential supply chain disruptions due to geopolitical tensions in the supplier's region. Emily recognized the urgent need to address this risk to prevent any operational interruptions.

Firstly, she conducted a detailed analysis of the supplier's situation, assessing the likelihood and potential duration of the disruption. She also explored the financial impact on the company if the supplier could not deliver the raw materials for an extended period. This analysis revealed significant vulnerabilities, highlighting the importance of immediate action.

Emily's first mitigation strategy was to identify alternative suppliers. She tasked the procurement team with finding and vetting new suppliers that could provide the same quality raw material. This process involved negotiating contracts and ensuring that these suppliers could meet the company's volume requirements. Establishing relationships with multiple suppliers diversified the risk, ensuring that the company wouldn't be overly dependent on any single source.

In addition to diversifying suppliers, Emily negotiated flexible contract terms with the primary supplier. These terms included clauses for price adjustment and delivery schedules in case of geopolitical disruptions. By having these contingencies in place, the company could better manage the financial impact of any supply chain issues.

Emily also implemented a hedging strategy to manage the financial risk associated with raw material price volatility. By entering into futures contracts, the company could lock in prices for the raw materials, thus stabilizing the cost structure. This hedging strategy provided a financial buffer against market fluctuations, ensuring that the company's profit margins remained protected.

To further safeguard against supply chain disruptions, Emily invested in increasing the company's inventory levels of the critical raw material. While this required a significant upfront cost, it provided a crucial buffer that could keep production running smoothly in case of any short-term supply issues. This decision was backed by a thorough cost-benefit analysis that balanced the carrying costs of additional inventory against the potential financial losses from operational downtime.

Emily also utilized insurance to transfer some of the supply chain risks. She reviewed and updated the company's business interruption insurance policy to ensure it covered losses due to supply chain disruptions. This insurance policy would provide financial compensation if the company faced significant operational downtime due to the unavailability of raw materials.

To maintain liquidity, Emily ensured the company had access to sufficient working capital. She negotiated lines of credit with the company's bank, providing a financial safety net that could be drawn upon in times of cash flow shortages. This proactive approach ensured that the company could meet its short-term financial obligations even during periods of supply chain instability.

Regular communication with all stakeholders was vital throughout this process. Emily kept the senior management team and the board of directors informed about the potential risks and the steps being taken to mitigate them. This transparency helped build confidence and ensured that everyone was aligned with the risk management strategy. Furthermore, she involved the procurement, finance, and operations teams in the decision-making process, ensuring that their insights and expertise were integrated into the risk mitigation plans.

Monitoring the effectiveness of these strategies was an ongoing task. Emily established key performance indicators (KPIs) to track supplier performance, inventory levels, and the financial impact of hedging activities. These KPIs were reviewed regularly, and any deviations from expected results prompted a reassessment of the mitigation strategies. For instance, if a new supplier failed to meet delivery schedules consistently, Emily would reevaluate the supplier's reliability and consider alternative options.

Another critical aspect of Emily's risk management approach was continuous improvement. She recognized that the risk landscape is dynamic, with new risks emerging over time. To stay ahead of potential threats, Emily implemented a process for regular risk reviews and updates. This involved periodic reassessments of the company's risk profile, incorporating changes in market conditions, geopolitical developments, and internal business dynamics. By staying vigilant and proactive, Emily ensured that the company's risk management strategies remained relevant and effective.

Emily's efforts in identifying and mitigating financial risks paid off when geopolitical tensions in the supplier's region escalated, leading to a temporary halt in raw material deliveries. Thanks to the diversified supplier base, increased inventory levels, and flexible contract terms, the company was able to continue its operations without significant disruptions. The financial impact of the raw material price volatility was also minimized due to the hedging strategies in place. Moreover, the business interruption insurance provided additional financial support, helping the company navigate through the challenging period without severe financial strain.

In conclusion, effective risk management involves a systematic approach to identifying, evaluating, and mitigating financial risks. By conducting thorough risk assessments, prioritizing risks based on their impact and likelihood, and developing comprehensive mitigation strategies, companies can safeguard their financial health and ensure business continuity. Diversification, hedging, insurance, strong internal controls, and continuous monitoring are all essential components of a robust risk management framework. Emily's proactive and strategic approach to risk management not only protected her company from potential financial losses but also positioned it for sustainable growth and resilience in an uncertain world.